CITIZEN JEFFERSON

CITIZEN JEFFERSON

The Wit and Wisdom of an
American Sage

Compiled and Edited by
JOHN P. KAMINSKI

MADISON HOUSE
Madison 1994

Kaminski, John P.

CITIZEN JEFFERSON
The Wit and Wisdom of an American Sage

Copyright © 1994 by Madison House Publishers, Inc.
All rights reserved.

LIBRARY OF CONGRESS CATALOGING-IN-PUBLICATION DATA

Citizen Jefferson : the wit and wisdom of an American sage /
compiled and edited by John P. Kaminski. — 1st ed.
p.   cm.
Includes index.
ISBN 0-945612-35-4 (acid-free : cloth). —
ISBN 0-945612-36-2 (acid-free : paper)
1. Jefferson, Thomas, 1743–1826—Quotations.
I. Kaminski, John P.
E302.J442   1994   93–40661
973.4'6'092—dc20   CIP

Typeset in Janson and Caslon
Designed by William Kasdorf

Printed in the United States of America
on acid-free paper by Edwards Brothers, Inc.

Published by
MADISON HOUSE PUBLISHERS, INC.
P. O. Box 3100
Madison, Wisconsin 53704

CONTENTS

For my mother-in-law
Martha Westaby

Who has throughout her life
epitomized Thomas Jefferson's ideal
of a kind and generous person.

INTRODUCTION

F ROM THE VERY BEGINNING of Jefferson's public
career, his ability to write was clear. His fiery
and eloquent pamphlet *A Summary View of the Rights
of British America* published in 1774 established
Jefferson's intercolonial reputation as a writer. Two
years later in the Second Continental Congress, it
seemed logical to place primary responsibility on the
thirty-three-year-old Virginian for the writing of the
most important document in American history. Some
might have thought the wise, old sage Benjamin
Franklin or the New England firebrand John Adams
should write the declaration establishing America's
independence; but, according to Adams, Jefferson
had "the reputation of a masterly pen . . . and a happy
talent of composition." In particular, the young Virginia congressman had a "peculiar felicity of expression."

Jefferson believed that "style in writing or speaking is formed very early in life while the imagination
is warm." As in other areas of life, he made it a point
not to follow the mainstream. Jefferson was not "a
friend to a scrupulous purism of style." He "readily
sacrifice[d] the niceties of syntax to euphony and

strength" and boldly abandoned "the rigorisms of grammar." He took care to find apt metaphors and craft eloquent turns of phrase. He also made it a point to preserve his correspondence, partly for history's sake, partly to defend earlier political stances, and partly because he recycled metaphors, allusions, and phrases from his earlier letters into later correspondence.

In all of his writing—and particularly in his private correspondence—Jefferson felt a responsibility to be interesting and eloquent. He succeeded remarkably well. His letters often read more like those of a novelist and sometimes even a poet. Maria Cosway, the beautiful, intelligent, and talented English landscape artist, wrote Jefferson that "when I read your letters they are so well wrote, so full of a thousand pretty things that it is not possible for me to answer such charming letters. I could say many things if my pen could write exactly my sentiments and feelings, but my letters must appear sad scrawls to you."

Only on three occasions did Jefferson's correspondence falter, primarily because the concerns of public business put tremendous pressure on his time. Jefferson's correspondence lagged while he served as governor of Virginia (1779–1781), secretary of state (1790–1793), and as president (1801–1809). The secretary of state complained to his grandson that "an eternal hurry of business prevents me from thinking" of anything of a private nature. Jefferson felt "like a horse under whip and spur from the start to the poll, without time to look to the right or left, my mind eternally forbidden to turn, even for a moment, to anything agreeable or useful to myself or family." While in France (1784–1789) and in retirement, however, Jefferson's writing excelled. His absence from home and friends while in France and his leisure and abandonment of politics after the presidency allowed Jefferson to fine-tune his letter writing.

Jefferson's correspondence falls into several distinct categories. Letters written to his daughters Martha and Mary as well as letters written to nephews, grandchildren, and young men seeking legal instruction and guidance are filled with the admonitions of a well-meaning parent and teacher. Letters to Maria Cosway flow with the passion of an absent lover and clearly show that Mrs. Cosway was the only woman other than his wife whom Jefferson loved romantically. Scholarly correspondence evinces Jefferson's respect for knowledge and inquisitiveness about the physical laws and secrets of the universe. His political correspondence ranges from the warm letters to friends such as James Madison, the Marquis de LaFayette, Benjamin Rush, and William Short; the respectful letters to George Washington; and his formal letters to political enemies such as Alexander Hamilton. Above all, his eloquent correspondence with John and Abigail Adams stands out, especially the correspondence after their rapprochement in 1812, which continued until Abigail died in 1818 and John Adams and Jefferson both died on the Fourth of July 1826—the fiftieth anniversary of the adoption of the Declaration of Independence.

The selections in this book reflect Jefferson's broad interests and keen insight into human nature. All of them have relevance today. The selections dealing with African Americans and Indians are particularly poignant and demonstrate that Jefferson shared some of the common bigotry of his contemporaries. Jefferson was aware of the prejudices of whites and the provocations against Indians and blacks, but he could see no future for Indians unless they were assimilated into white society; he could only hope for the emancipation of black slaves if they were separated from whites by a policy of forced colonization. His attitudes on these matters help explain why the Founding Fathers could not solve their most difficult social problem and why racism still plagues us today. Thus, even in those areas where Jefferson stumbled, he can be instructive.

꽃 꽃

A number of sources have been extremely helpful in gathering the selections in this book. *The Papers of Thomas Jefferson* edited in succession by Julian P. Boyd, Charles T. Cullen, and John Catanzariti has been my primary source. Beyond these volumes, I have also used the Paul Leicester Ford and the H. A. Washington editions of Jefferson's writings, Lester J. Cappon's edition of *The Adams–Jefferson Letters*, Bernard Mayo's *Jefferson Himself*, and the Library of America's edition of Jefferson's *Writings* compiled by Merrill D. Peterson. John P. Foley's *Jefferson Cyclopedia* (New York, 1900) has also been helpful but must be used cautiously because the compiler altered many of Jefferson's passages.

Whenever possible, selections in *Citizen Jefferson* were checked against the original manuscript letters in the Library of Congress and the University of Virginia microfilm editions. Except for minor changes in spelling and the capitalization of the first letters in sentences (which Jefferson usually did not do), the text is faithful to the original. Attributions for each selection give the name of the recipient, the place from where Jefferson wrote his letters, and the date of writing.

A number of people have assisted me. Using my draft manuscript, Nancy J. Taylor, a graduate student at the University of Wisconsin, made copies of the relevant pages of the original letters from the Jefferson microfilm. She highlighted all of the relevant passages, making it easy for me to check the accuracy of my transcriptions. Five friends—Gregory M. Britton, Paul Hass, William Kasdorf, Richard Leffler, and Ann Windsor—read the manuscript and offered their advice as to which selections should be kept, shortened, or deleted. Their advice was enormously helpful. My colleague Gaspare J. Saladino suggested the title *Citizen Jefferson* and recommended that the design used for a previous book, *A Great and Good Man*, be adapted to this volume. As in the past, my wife Janice has been extremely patient and encouraging, allowing me to devote the long evening hours and week-ends necessary to complete this project. Finally, it was but a short time into this book that I realized that *Citizen Jefferson* would be dedicated to my mother-in-law Martha Westaby. The whole world and I feel toward Martha the way Jefferson felt toward his daughter Mary: "Take more pleasure in giving what is best to another than in having it yourself, and then all the world will love you, and I more than all the world." Martha Westaby is truly loved by everyone she has touched.

Thomas Jefferson Chronology

✠ ✠

1743–1826

1743	Born at Shadwell, Virginia (April 13)
1760–1762	Student at the College of William and Mary
1762–1767	Period of self-education and preparation for the law
1769–1774	Delegate in Virginia House of Burgesses
1772	Marries Martha Wayles Skelton (January 1)
1774	Writes *A Summary View of the Rights of British America*
1775–1776	Delegate to Second Continental Congress
1776	Drafts Declaration of Independence
1776–1779	Delegate in Virginia House of Delegates
1779	Submits Bill for Establishing Religious Freedom
1779–1781	Governor of Virginia
1781–1782	Writes Notes on the State of Virginia
1782	Death of wife (September 6)
1783–1784	Delegate to Confederation Congress
1784–1789	U.S. Minister Plenipotentiary to France
1790–1793	U.S. Secretary of State
1797–1801	Vice President of the United States
1801–1809	President of the United States
1804	Death of daughter Mary (April 17)
1814–1826	Establishes the University of Virginia
1826	Dies at Monticello (July 4)

THE WORDS OF
JEFFERSON

Advice

The greatest favor which can be done me is the communication of the opinions of judicious men, of men who do not suffer their judgments to be biassed by either interest or passions.

To Chandler Price, Washington, February 28, 1807

How easily we prescribe for others a cure for their difficulties, while we cannot cure our own.

To John Adams, Monticello, January 22, 1821

Adore God. Reverence and cherish your parents. Love your neighbor as yourself, and your country more than yourself. Be just. Be true. Murmur not at the ways of Providence.

To Thomas Jefferson Smith, Monticello, February 21, 1825

African Americans

No body wishes more than I do to see such proofs as you exhibit, that nature has given to our black brethren, talents equal to those of the other colours of men, & that the appearance of a want of them is owing merely to the degraded condition of their existence both in Africa & America. I can add with truth that no body wishes more ardently to see a good system commenced for raising the condition both of their body & mind to what it ought to be, as fast as the imbecillity of their present existence, and other circumstances which cannot be neglected, will admit.

To Benjamin Banneker, Philadelphia, August 30, 1791

Agriculture

Those who labor in the earth are the chosen people of god, if ever he had a chosen people, whose breasts he has made his peculiar deposit for substantial and genuine virtue.

Notes on the State of Virginia, 1782

Cultivators of the earth are the most valuable citizens. They are the most vigorous, the most independent, the most virtuous, & they are tied to their country & wedded to its liberty & interests by the most lasting bands.

To John Jay, Paris, August 23, 1785

America

The station which we occupy among the nations of the earth is honorable, but awful. Trusted with the destinies of this solitary republic of the world, the only monument of human rights, & the sole depository of the sacred fire of freedom & self-government from hence it is to be lighted up in other regions of the earth, if other regions of the earth shall ever become susceptible of its benign influence. All mankind ought then, with us, to rejoice in its prosperous, & sympathize in its adverse fortunes, as involving every thing dear to man.

To the Citizens of Washington, March 4, 1809

It is a part of the American character to consider nothing as desperate; to surmount every difficulty by resolution and contrivance. In Europe there are shops for every want. Its inhabitants therefore have no idea that their wants can be furnished otherwise. Remote from all other aid, we are obliged to invent and to execute; to find means within ourselves, and not to lean on others.

To Martha Jefferson, Aix en Provence, March 28, 1787

There is a modesty often which does itself injury. Our countrymen possess this. They do not know their own superiority.

To John Rutledge, Jr., Paris, February 2, 1788

Never was a finer canvas presented to work on than our countrymen. All of them engaged in agriculture or the pursuits of honest industry, independent in their circumstances, enlightened as to their rights, and firm in their habits of order & obedience to the laws. This I hope will be the age of experiments in government, and that their basis will be founded in principles of honesty, not of mere force. We have seen no instance of this since the days of the Roman republic, nor do we read of any before that.

To John Adams, Monticello, February 28, 1796

The Arts

You see I am an enthusiast on the subject of the arts. But it is an enthusiasm of which I am not ashamed, as its object is to improve the taste of my countrymen, to increase their reputation, to reconcile to them the respect of the world & procure them its praise.

To James Madison, Paris, September 20, 1785

Bad Timing

A good cause is often injured more by ill timed efforts of its friends than by the arguments of its enemies.

To James Heaton, Monticello, May 20, 1826

Bigotry

Bigotry is the disease of ignorance, of morbid minds; enthusiasm of the free and buoyant. Education & free discussion are the antidotes of both.

To John Adams, Monticello, August 1, 1816

Ignorance & bigotry, like other insanities, are incapable of self-government.

To Marquis de LaFayette, Monticello, May 14, 1817

Bill of Rights

A bill of rights is what the people are entitled to against every government on earth, general or particular, & what no just government should refuse or rest on inferences.

To James Madison, Paris, December 20, 1787

Blessings of Life

The good things of this life are scattered so sparingly in our way that we must glean them up as we go.

To Abigail Adams, Paris, November 1786

Books

Read good books because they will encourage as well as direct your feelings.

To Peter Carr, Paris, August 10, 1787

I cannot live without books.

To John Adams, Monticello, June 10, 1815

Botany

※ ※

Botany I rank with the most valuable sciences, whether we consider its subjects as furnishing the principal subsistence of life to man & beast, delicious varieties for our tables, refreshments from our orchards, the adornments of our flower-borders, shade and perfume of our groves, materials for our buildings, or medicaments for our bodies.

To Thomas Cooper, Monticello, October 7, 1814

Character

※ ※

The uniform tenor of a man's life furnishes better evidence of what he has said or done on any particular occasion than the word of any enemy.

To George Clinton, Washington, December 31, 1803

Charity

※ ※

I deem it the duty of every man to devote a certain proportion of his income for charitable purposes. . . . However disposed the mind may feel to unlimited good, our means having limits, we are necessarily circumscribed by them.

To Drs. Rogers and Slaughter, Washington, March 2, 1806

Private charities, as well as contributions to public purposes in proportion to every one's circumstances, are certainly among the duties we owe to society.

To Charles Christian, Monticello, March 21, 1812

A Child's Illness

Doctors always flatter, and parents always fear. It remains to see which is right.

To Martha Jefferson Carr, Philadelphia, April 14, 1793

Christianity

I am a *real Christian*; that is to say, a disciple of the doctrines of Jesus.

To Charles Thomson, Monticello, January 9, 1816

Cities

The mobs of great cities add just so much to the support of pure government, as sores do to the strength of the human body.

Notes on the State of Virginia, 1782

I view great cities as pestilential to the morals, the health and the liberties of man.

To Benjamin Rush, Monticello, September 23, 1800

Climate

Certainly it is a truth that climate is one of the sources of the greatest sensual enjoyment.

To Joseph Priestley, Washington, June 19, 1802

Coercion

What has been the effect of coercion? To make one half the world fools, and the other half hypocrites.

Notes on the State of Virginia, 1782

Cold Weather

I have no doubt but that cold is the source of more sufferance to all animal nature than hunger, thirst, sickness & all the other pains of life & death itself put together.

To William Dunbar, Washington, January 12, 1801

Commerce

It should be our endeavor to cultivate the peace and friendship of every nation. . . . Our interest will be to throw open the doors of commerce, and to knock off all its shackles, giving perfect freedom to all persons for the vent of whatever they may choose to bring into our ports, and asking the same in theirs.

Notes on the State of Virginia, 1782

Common Sense

I can never fear that things will go far wrong where common sense has fair play.

To John Adams, Paris, December 20, 1786

Let common sense & common honesty have fair play & they will soon set things to rights.

To Ezra Stiles, Paris, December 24, 1786

There are no mysteries in it. Difficulties indeed sometimes arise; but common sense and honest intentions will generally steer thro' them.

To Josephus B. Stuart, Monticello, May 10, 1817

Condolences

I . . . sincerely condole with you on the great loss you have sustained. Experience, however, in the same bitter school has taught me that it is not condolence, but time and silence alone which can heal those wounds.

To Henry Remsen, Philadelphia, March 18, 1792

Condolences were but renewals of grief.

To Benjamin Rush, Monticello, January 16, 1811

Tried myself, in the school of affliction, by the loss of every form of connection which can rive the human heart, I know well, and feel what you have lost, what you have suffered, are suffering, and have yet to endure. The same trials have taught me that, for ills so immeasureable, time and silence are the only medicines. I will not therefore, by useless condolances, open afresh the sluices of your grief nor, altho' mingling sincerely my tears with yours, will I say a word more, where words are vain, but that it is of some comfort to us both that the term is not very distant at which we are to deposit, in the same cerement, our sorrows and suffering bodies, and to ascend in essence to an ecstatic meeting with the friends we have loved and lost and whom we shall still love and never lose again. God bless you and support you under your heavy affliction.

To John Adams, Monticello, November 13, 1818
On the death of Abigail Adams

Confidence

We confide in our own strength, without boasting of it; we respect that of others, without fearing it.

To William Carmichael and William Short,
Philadelphia, June 30, 1793

Congress

If there be any thing amiss therefore, in the present state of our affairs, as the formidable deficit lately unfolded to us indicates, I ascribe it to the inattention of Congress to its duties, to their unwise dissipation & waste of the public contributions. They seemed, some little while ago to be at a loss for objects whereon to throw away the supposed fathomless funds of the treasury.

To Thomas Ritchie, Monticello, December 25, 1820

Conscience

Never do nor say a bad thing. If ever you are about to say any thing amiss or to do any thing wrong, consider before hand. You will feel something within you which will tell you it is wrong & ought not to be said or done: this is your conscience, & be sure to obey it. Our maker has given us all, this faithful internal Monitor, and if you always obey it, you will always be prepared for the end of the world: or for a much more certain event which is death. This must happen to all: it puts an end to the world as to us, & the way to be ready for it is never to do a wrong act.

To Martha Jefferson, Annapolis, December 11, 1783

The moral sense, or conscience, is as much a part of man as his leg or arm. It is given to all human beings in a stronger or weaker degree, as force of members is given them in a greater or less degree. It may be strengthened by exercise, as may any particular limb of the body. This sense is submitted indeed in some degree to the guidance of reason; but it is a small stock which is required for this: even a less one than what we call Common sense. State a moral case to a ploughman & a professor. The former will decide it as well, & often better than the latter, because he has not been led astray by artificial rules.

The Constitution

I join cordially in admiring and revering the Constitution of the United States, the result of the collected wisdom of our country. That wisdom has committed to us the important task of proving by example that a government, if organized in all its parts on the Representative principle unadulterated by the infusion of spurious elements, if founded, not in the fears & follies of man, but on his reason, on his sense of right, on the predominance of the social over his dissocial passions, may be so free as to restrain him in no moral right, and so firm as to protect him from every moral wrong.

To Amos Marsh, Washington, November 20, 1801

Tho' written constitutions may be violated in moments of passion or delusion, yet they furnish a text to which those who are watchful may again rally & recall the people: they fix too for the people the principles for their political creed.

To Joseph Priestley, Washington, June 19, 1802

Our peculiar security is in possession of a written constitution. Let us not make it a blank paper by construction.

To Wilson Cary Nicholas, Monticello, September 7, 1803

Conversation

An hour of conversation would be worth a volume of letters.

To John Adams, Monticello, April 8, 1816

Conviction

A conviction that we are right accomplishes half the difficulty of correcting wrong.

To Archibald Thweat, Monticello, January 19, 1821

Correspondence

But why has no body else written to me? Is it that one is forgotten as soon as their back is turned? I have a better opinion of men. It must be either that they think that the details known to themselves are known to every body and so come to us thro' a thousand channels, or that we should set no value on them. Nothing can be more erroneous than both those opinions. We value those details, little and great, public and private, in proportion to our distance from our own country: and so far are they from getting to us through a thousand channels, that we hear no more of them or of our country here than if we were among the dead.

To James Monroe, Paris, April 15, 1785

The drudgery of letter-writing often denies the leisure of reading a single page in a week.

To Ezra Stiles, Monticello, June 25, 1819

A line from my good old friends is like balm to my soul.

To Nathaniel Macon, Monticello, November 23, 1821

Courage

Our captain is as bold a sailor as a judicious one should be.

To Nathaniel Cutting, Lynhaven Bay, November 21, 1789
After arriving safely in Virginia from Europe

Curiosity

Man . . . is in all his shapes a curious animal.

To C. F. C. de Volney, Monticello, January 8, 1797

Cynicism

There is no act, however virtuous, for which ingenuity may not find some bad motive.

To Edward Dowse, Washington, April 19, 1803

Death

There is a fulness of time when men should go, & not occupy too long the ground to which others have a right to advance.

To Benjamin Rush, Monticello, August 17, 1811

There is a ripeness of time for death, regarding others as well as ourselves, when it is reasonable we should drop off, and make room for another growth. When we have lived our generation out, we should not wish to encroach on another.

To John Adams, Monticello, August 1, 1816

Mine is the next turn, and I shall meet it with good will, for after one's friends are all gone before them, and our faculties leaving us, too, one by one, why wish to linger in mere vegetation—as a solitary trunk in a desolate field, from which all its former companions have disappeared?

To Maria Cosway, Monticello, December 27, 1820

Decalogue of Canons for Observation in Practical Life

1. Never put off till tomorrow what you can do to-day.
2. Never trouble another for what you can do yourself.
3. Never spend your money before you have it.
4. Never buy what you do not want, because it is cheap; it will be dear to you.
5. Pride costs us more than hunger, thirst and cold.
6. We never repent of having eaten too little.
7. Nothing is troublesome that we do willingly.
8. How much pain have cost us the evils which have never happened.
9. Take things always by their smooth handle.
10. When angry, count ten, before you speak; if very angry, an hundred.

To Thomas Jefferson Smith, Monticello, February 21, 1825

Defamation

🎋 🎋

Defamation is becoming a necessary of life; insomuch that a dish of tea, in the morning or evening, cannot be digested without this stimulant. Even those who do not believe these abominations, still read them with complacence to their auditors, and instead of the abhorrence & indignation which should fill a virtuous mind, betray a secret pleasure in the possibility that some may believe them, tho they do not themselves. It seems to escape them that it is not he who prints, but he who pays for printing a slander, who is its real author.

To John Norvell, Washington, June 11, 1807

Defense

🎋 🎋

Weakness provokes insult & injury, while a condition to punish it often prevents it.

To Secretary for Foreign Affairs John Jay, Paris, August 23, 1785

I am satisfied the good sense of the people is the strongest army our governments can ever have, & that it will not fail them.

To William Carmichael, Paris, December 26, 1786

Whatever enables us to go to war, secures our peace.

To James Monroe, New York, July 11, 1790

Were armies to be raised whenever a speck of war is visible in our horizon, we never should have been without them. Our resources would have been exhausted on dangers which have never happened, instead of being reserved for what is really to take place.

Sixth Annual Message, December 2, 1806

Delegation of Authority

There is no delegating a trust by halves.

To Alexander Donald, Philadelphia, November 25, 1790

Democracy

Every government degenerates when trusted to the rulers of the people alone. The people themselves therefore are its only safe depositories.

Notes on the State of Virginia, 1782

It is an axiom in my mind that our liberty can never be safe but in the hands of the people themselves, & that too of the people with a certain degree of instruction.

To George Washington, Paris, January 4, 1786

Sometimes it is said that man cannot be trusted with the government of himself. Can he, then, be trusted with the government of others? Or have we found angels in the forms of kings to govern him? Let history answer this question.

First Inaugural Address, March 4, 1801

The government which can wield the arm of the people must be the strongest possible.

To Mr. Weaver, Washington, June 7, 1807

Where the Law of the majority ceases to be acknowledged, there government ends, the Law of the strongest takes its place, & life & property are his who can take them.

To John Gassway, Washington, February 17, 1809

What a germ have we planted, and how faithfully should we cherish the parent tree at home!

To Benjamin Austin, Monticello, January 9, 1816

We of the United States, you know are constitutionally & conscientiously Democrats.

To P. S. Dupont de Nemours, Poplar Forest, April 24, 1816

I know no safe depository of the ultimate powers of the society but the people themselves: and if we think them not enlightened enough to exercise their controul with a wholsome discretion, the remedy is not to take it from them, but to inform their discretion by education. This is the true corrective of abuses of constitutional power.

To William Charles Jarvis, Monticello, September 28, 1820

The general spread of the light of science has already laid open to every view the palpable truth that the mass of mankind has not been born, with saddles on their backs, nor a favored few booted and spurred, ready to ride them legitimately, by the grace of god.

To Roger C. Weightman, Monticello, June 24, 1826

Dependence

Dependence begets subservience and venality, suffocates the germ of virtue, and prepares fit tools for the designs of ambition.

Notes on the State of Virginia, *1782*

Difficulties

Calamity was our best physician.

To Richard Price, Paris, February 1, 1785

Diplomacy

Circumstances sometimes require that rights the most unquestionable should be advanced with delicacy.

To William Short, Philadelphia, July 28, 1791

Disputes

In little disputes with your companions, give way rather than insist on trifles, for their love and the approbation of others will be worth more to you than the trifle in dispute.

To Francis Eppes, Monticello, May 21, 1816
Instructions to Jefferson's young grandson

Doubt

In cases of doubt it is better to say too little than too much.

To President George Washington, Philadelphia, July 30, 1791

Dreams

My theory has always been that if we are to dream, the flatteries of hope are as cheap, and pleasanter than the gloom of despair.

To François de Marbois, Monticello, June 14, 1817

Mine, after all, may be an Utopian dream; but being innocent, I have thought I might indulge in it till I go to the land of dreams, and sleep there with the dreamers of all past and future times.

To J. Correa de Serra, Poplar Forest, November 25, 1817

Duty

There is a debt of service due from every man to his country, proportioned to the bounties which nature & fortune have measured to him.

To Edward Rutledge, Monticello, December 27, 1796

Some men are born for the public. Nature, by fitting them for the service of the human race on a broad scale, has stamped them with the evidences of her destination & their duty.

To James Monroe, Washington, January 13, 1803

The first of all our consolations is that of having faithfully fulfilled our duties; the next, the approbation & good will of those who have witnessed it.

To James Fishback, Monticello, September 27, 1809

We have been thrown into times of a peculiar character, and to work our way through them has required services & sacrifices from our countrymen generally, and, to their great honor, these have been generally exhibited, by every one in his sphere, & according to the opportunities afforded. With them I have been a fellow laborer, endeavoring to do faithfully the part allotted to me, as they did theirs; & it is a subject of mutual congratulation that, in a state of things, such as the world had never before seen, we have gotten on so far well: and my confidence in our present high functionaries, as well as in my countrymen generally leaves me without much fear for the future.

To James Fishback, Monticello, September 27, 1809

Economy

There is no man who has not some vice or folly the atoning of which would not pay his taxes.

To James Madison, Annapolis, May 8, 1784

The multiplication of public offices, increase of expense beyond income, growth and entailment of a public debt, are indications soliciting the employment of the pruning-knife.

To Spencer Roane, Monticello, March 9, 1821

Education

The bulk of mankind are school boys thro' life.

Notes on Coinage, Annapolis, March-May 1784

The boys of the rising generation are to be the men of the next, and the sole guardians of the principles we deliver over to them.

To Samuel Knox, Monticello, February 12, 1810

Enlighten the people generally, and tyranny and oppressions of body & mind will vanish like evil spirits at the dawn of day.

To P. S. Dupont de Nemours, Poplar Forest, April 24, 1816

If the condition of man is to be progressively ameliorated, as we fondly hope & believe, education is to be the chief instrument in effecting it.

To M. Jullien, Monticello, July 23, 1818

That every man shall be made virtuous, by any process whatever, is indeed no more to be expected, than that every tree shall be made to bear fruit, and every plant nourishment. The briar and bramble can never become the vine and olive; but their asperities may be softened by culture, and their properties improved to usefulness in the order and economy of the world.

To Cornelius Camden Blatchly, Monticello, October 21, 1822

Employment

义 义

Interesting occupations are essential to happiness: indeed the whole art of being happy consists in the art of finding employment.

To Martha Jefferson Randolph, New York, April 26, 1790

Never fear the want of business. A man who qualifies himself well for his calling never fails of employment in it.

To Peter Carr, Philadelphia, June 22, 1792

End of the World

义 义

I hope you will have good sense enough to disregard those foolish predictions that the world is to be at an end soon. The almighty has never made known to any body at what time he created it, nor will he tell any body when he means to put an end to it, if ever he means to do it. As to preparations for that event, the best way is for you to be always prepared for it.

To Martha Jefferson, Annapolis, December 11, 1783

Enemies

An enemy generally says & believes what he wishes.

To C. W. F. Dumas, Paris, March 29, 1788

An injured friend is the bitterest of foes.

Opinion on the French Treaties, April 28, 1793

England

Our laws, language, religion, politics, & manners are so deeply laid in English foundations, that we shall never cease to consider their history as a part of ours, and to study ours in that as its origin.

To William Duane, Monticello, August 12, 1810

No nation on earth can hurt us so much as yours; none be more useful to you than ours.

To William Roscoe, Monticello, December 27, 1820

Error

The errors and misfortunes of others should be a school for our own instruction.

To Mary Jefferson Eppes, Philadelphia, January 7, 1798

Time and truth will at length correct error.

To C.F.C. de Volney, Washington, February 8, 1805

Error is the stuff of which the web of life is woven: and he who lives longest and wisest is only able to weave out the more of it.

To François J. de Chastellux, Paris, October 1786

Evil

It is a happy circumstance in human affairs that evils which are not cured in one way, will cure themselves in some other.

To Sir John Sinclair, Philadelphia, August 24, 1791

When great evils happen, I am in the habit of looking out for what good may arise from them as consolations to us; and Providence has in fact so established the order of things as that most evils are the means of producing some good.

To Benjamin Rush, Monticello, September 23, 1800

It is the melancholy law of human societies to be compelled sometimes to choose a great evil in order to ward off a greater.

To William Short, Monticello, November 28, 1814

Example

I have ever deemed it more honorable, & more profitable too, to set a good example than to follow a bad one. The good opinion of mankind, like the lever of Archimedes, with the given fulcrum, moves the world.

To J. Correa de Serra, Monticello, December 27, 1814

Exercise

The sovereign invigorator of the body is exercise.

To Thomas Mann Randolph, Jr., Paris, August 27, 1786

Exercise and application produce order in our affairs, health of body, chearfulness of mind, and these make us precious to our friends.

To Martha Jefferson, Aix en Provence, March 28, 1787

Expedience

🦋 🦋

The mind of man is full of expedients.

To the Comte de Moustier, Paris, May 20, 1789

Experience

🦋 🦋

The ground I have already passed over enables me to see my way into that which is before me.

To George Washington, Chesterfield, December 15, 1789

But all theory must yield to experience, and every constitution has its own laws.

To James Maury, Monticello, June 16, 1815

Yet experience & frequent disappointment have taught me not to be over-confident in theories or calculations, until actual trial of the whole combination has stamped it with approbation.

To George Fleming, Monticello, December 29, 1815

Forty years of experience in government is worth a century of book-reading.

To Samuel Kercheval, Monticello, July 12, 1816

Fame

He is happiest of whom the world says least, good or bad.

To John Adams, Paris, August 27, 1786

Familiarity

By analyzing too minutely we often reduce our subject to atoms of which the mind loses its hold.

To Edward Everett, Monticello, February 24, 1823

Family

The happiest moments of my life have been the few which I have past at home in the bosom of my family.

To Francis Willis, Jr., New York, April 18, 1790

I have here company enough, part of which is very friendly, part well enough disposed, part secretly hostile, and a constant succession of strangers. But this only serves to get rid of life, not to enjoy it; it is in the love of one's family only that heartfelt happiness is known. I feel it when we are all together, and, when alone, beyond what can be imagined.

To Mary Jefferson Eppes, Washington, October 26, 1801

Fatherhood

To be a good husband and a good father at this moment you must be also a good citizen.

To Elbridge Gerry, Philadelphia, June 21, 1797

Favors

Those who have had, and who may yet have occasion to ask favors, should never ask small ones.

To Marquis de Lafayette, Paris, June 15, 1786

Force

With every barbarous people . . . force is law.

Notes on the State of Virginia, 1782

Force cannot change right.

To John Cartwright, Monticello, June 5, 1824

Foreign Relations

We certainly cannot deny to other nations that principle whereon our own government is founded, that every nation has a right to govern itself internally under what forms it pleases, and to change these forms at its own will: and externally to transact business with other nations thro' whatever organ it chuses, whether that be a king, convention, assembly, committee, president, or whatever it be. The only thing essential is the will of the nation.

To Thomas Pinckney, Philadelphia, December 30, 1792

Commerce with all nations, alliance with none should be our motto.

To Thomas Lomax, Monticello, March 12, 1799

Peace, commerce and honest friendship with all nations, entangling alliances with none.

First Inaugural Address, 1801

Formalities

It would be ridiculous in the present case to talk about forms. There are situations when form must be dispensed with. A man attacked by assassins will call for help to those nearest him, & will not think himself bound to silence till a magistrate may come to his aid.

To William Short, Philadelphia, November 24, 1791

Fortitude

Fortitude . . . teaches us to meet and surmount difficulties; not to fly from them, like cowards, and to fly too in vain, for they will meet and arrest us at every turn of our road.

To William Short, Monticello, October 31, 1819

France

Ask the travelled inhabitant of any nation, In what country on earth would you rather live?—Certainly in my own, where all my friends, my relations, and the earliest & sweetest affections and recollections of my life. Which would be your second choice? France.

Autobiography, 1821

Frankness

Half-confidences are not in my character.

To Elbridge Gerry, Philadelphia, January 26, 1799

Freedom

The human mind will some day get back to the freedom it enjoyed 2000 years ago. This country, which has given to the world the example of physical liberty, owes to it that of moral emancipation also. For, as yet, it is but nominal with us. The inquisition of public opinion overwhelms in practice the freedom asserted by the laws in theory.

To John Adams, Monticello, January 22, 1821

Freedom of the Press

No experiment can be more interesting than that we are now trying, & which we trust will end in establishing the fact that man may be governed by reason and truth. Our first object should therefore be to leave open to him all the avenues to truth. The most effectual hitherto found is the freedom of the press.

To John Tyler, Washington, June 28, 1804

Our liberty depends on the freedom of the press, and that cannot be limited without being lost.

To Dr. James Currie, Paris, January 28, 1786

No government ought to be without censors: & where the press is free, no one ever will.

To George Washington, Monticello, September 9, 1792

The press, confined to truth, needs no other legal restraint; the public judgment will correct false reasonings and opinions, on a full hearing of all parties; and no other definite line can be drawn between the inestimable liberty of the press and its demoralizing licentiousness.

Second Inaugural Address, March 4, 1805

Friends

※ ※

Agreeable society is the first essential in constituting the happiness & of course the value of our existence: & it is a circumstance worthy great attention when we are making first our choice of a residence.

To James Madison, Paris, December 8, 1784

It seems as if, our ancient friends dying off, the whole mass of the affections of the heart survives undiminished to the few who remain.

To Elbridge Gerry, Monticello, June 11, 1812

Friendship

※ ※

Life is of no value but as it brings us gratifications. Among the most valuable of these is rational society. It informs the mind, sweetens the temper, cheers our spirits, and promotes health.

To James Madison, Annapolis, February 20, 1784

THE HEAD SPEAKING

Friendship is but another name for an alliance with the follies & the misfortunes of others. Our own share of miseries is sufficient: why enter then as volunteers into those of another? Is there so little gall poured into our own cup that we must needs help to

39

drink that of our neighbor? A friend dies or leaves us: we feel as if a limb was cut off. He is sick: we must watch over him, & participate of his pains. His fortune is shipwrecked; ours must be laid under contribution. He loses a child, a parent or a partner: we must mourn the loss as if it was our own.

THE HEART SPEAKING

What more sublime delight than to mingle tears with one whom the hand of heaven hath smitten! To watch over the bed of sickness, & to beguile its tedious & its painful moments! To share our bread with one to whom misfortune has left none! This world abounds indeed with misery; to lighten its burthen we must divide it with one another. . . . Friendship is precious, not only in the shade but in the sunshine of life: & thanks to a benevolent arrangement of things, the greater part of life is sunshine.

To Maria Cosway, Paris, October 12, 1786

The happiest moments it [my heart] knows are those in which it is pouring forth its affections to a few esteemed characters.

To Eliza House Trist, Paris, December 15, 1786

The friendships contracted earliest in life, are those which stand by us the longest.

To Elizabeth Blair Thompson, Paris, January 19, 1787

Near friends falling out never reunite cordially.

To Alexander Donald, Paris, February 7, 1788

Preserve for me always, my dear friend, the same sentiments of esteem you have been so good as to entertain for me hitherto. They will comfort me in going, and encourage me returning.

To Maria Cosway, Paris, September 11, 1789

Every human being, my dear, must thus be viewed according to what it is good for, for none of us, no not one, is perfect; and were we to love none who had imperfections this world would be a desert for our love. All we can do is to make the best of our friends: love and cherish what is good in them, and keep out of the way of what is bad: but no more think of rejecting them for it than of throwing away a piece of music for a flat passage or two.

To Martha Jefferson Randolph, New York, July 17, 1790

Trouble is a pleasure when it is to serve our friends living or dead.

To Elizabeth Wayles Eppes, Philadelphia, May 15, 1791

Friends we have if we have merited them. Those of our earliest years stand nearest in our affections.

To John Page, Washington, June 25, 1804

I find friendship to be like wine, raw when new, ripened with age, the true old man's milk & restorative cordial.

To Benjamin Rush, Monticello, August 17, 1811

The Future

I like the dreams of the future better than the history of the past.

To John Adams, Monticello, August 1, 1816

Gardening

I have often thought that if heaven had given me choice of my position & calling, it should have been on a rich spot of earth, well watered, and near a good market for the productions of the garden. No occupation is so delightful to me as the culture of the earth, & no culture comparable to that of the garden. Such a variety of subjects, some one always coming to perfection, the failure of one thing repaired by the success of another, & instead of one harvest, a continued one thro' the year. Under a total want of demand except for our family table. I am still devoted to the garden. But tho' an old man, I am but a young gardener.

To Charles Willson Peale, Poplar Forest, August 20, 1811

Generations

✻ ✻

That the earth belongs in usufruct to the living: that the dead have neither powers nor rights over it. The portion occupied by any individual ceases to be his when [he] himself ceases to be, & reverts to the society.

To James Madison, Paris, September 6, 1789

Nothing is more incumbent on the old, than to know when they should get out of the way, and relinquish to younger successors the honors they can no longer earn, and the duties they can no longer perform.

To John Vaughan, Monticello, February 5, 1815

It is a law of nature that the generations of men should give way, one to another, and I hope that the one now on the stage will preserve for their sons the political blessings delivered into their hands by their fathers. Time indeed changes manners and notions, and so far we must expect institutions to bend to them. But time produces also corruption of principles, and against this it is the duty of good citizens to be ever on the watch, and if the gangrene is to prevail at last, let the day be kept off as long as possible.

To Spencer Roane, Monticello, March 9, 1821

Generosity

Take more pleasure in giving what is best to another than in having it yourself, and then all the world will love you, and I more than all the world.

To Mary Jefferson, New York, April 11, 1790

Good Faith

Good faith is every man's surest guide.

Proclamation Announcing Peace Treaty, January 14, 1784

Good Humor

We had all rather associate with a good humored, light-principled man than with an ill tempered rigorist in morality.

To Benjamin Rush, Washington, January 3, 1808

Above all things, and at all times, practise yourself in good humor; this of all human qualities is the most amiable and endearing to society.

To Francis Eppes, Monticello, May 21, 1816

Governing

✣ ✣

I leave to others the sublime delights of riding in the storm, better pleased with sound sleep & a warmer berth below it encircled, with the society of neighbors, friends & fellow laborers of the earth rather than with spies & sycophants. . . . I have no ambition to govern men. It is a painful and thankless office.

To John Adams, Monticello, December 28, 1796

An honest man can feel no pleasure in the exercise of power over his fellow citizens. . . . There has never been a moment of my life in which I should have relinquished for it the enjoyments of my family, my farm, my friends & books.

To John Melish, Monticello, January 13, 1813

Government

✣ ✣

The whole art of government consists in the art of being honest.

A Summary of the Rights of British America, *May 1774*

The legitimate powers of government extend to such acts only as are injurious to others.

Notes on the State of Virginia, *1782*

The happiness & prosperity of our citizens . | . | . is the only legitimate object of government.

To Thaddeus Kosciusko, Monticello, April 16, 1811

The only orthodox object of the institution of government is to secure the greatest degree of happiness possible to the general mass of those associated under it.

To Francis A. Van Der Kemp, Monticello, March 22, 1812

The way to have good and safe government, is not to trust it all to one; but to divide it among the many, distributing to every one exactly the functions he is competent to. Let the National government be entrusted with the defence of the nation, and its foreign & federal relations; the State governments with the civil rights, laws, police & administration of what concerns the state generally; the Counties with the local concerns of the counties, and each Ward direct the interests within itself. It is by dividing and subdividing these republics from the great National one down thro' all its subordinations, until it ends in the administration of every man's farm and affairs by himself; by placing under every one what his own eye may superintend, that all will be done for the best.

To Joseph C. Cabell, Monticello, February 2, 1816

Grief

Deeply practised in the school of affliction, the human heart knows no joy which I have not lost, no sorrow of which I have not drunk! Fortune can present no grief of unknown form to me! Who then can so softly bind up the wound of another as he who has felt the same wound himself?

To Maria Cosway, Paris, October 12, 1786

I have ever found time & silence the only medecine, and these but assuage, they never can suppress, the deep-drawn sigh which recollection for ever brings up, until recollection and life are extinguished together.

To John Adams, Monticello, October 12, 1813

I have often wondered for what good end the sensations of Grief could be intended. All our other passions, within proper bounds, have an useful object. And the perfection of the moral character is, not in a Stoical apathy, so hypocritically vaunted, and so untruly too, because impossible; but in a just equilibrium of all the passions. I wish the pathologists then would tell us what is the use of grief in the economy, and of what good it is the cause, proximate or remote.

To John Adams, Monticello, April 8, 1816

Habits

꽃 꽃

I find as I advance in life I become less capable of acquiring new affections & therefore I love to hang by my old ones.

To Alexander Donald, Philadelphia, May 13, 1791

Half-Way Measures

Things which are just or handsome should never be done by halves.

To Benjamin Harrison, Paris, January 12, 1785

Happiness

Our greatest happiness . . . is always the result of a good conscience, good health, occupation, and freedom in all just pursuits.

Notes on the State of Virginia, 1782

My principal happiness is now in the retrospect of life.

To John Page, Paris, August 20, 1785

It is neither wealth nor splendor, but tranquility and occupation which give happiness.

To Anna Scott Jefferson Marks, Paris, July 12, 1788

Be assiduous in learning, take much exercise for your health & practise much virtue. Health, learning & virtue will ensure your happiness; they will give you a quiet conscience, private esteem & public honour. Beyond these we want nothing but physical necessaries; and they are easily obtained.

To Peter Carr, Paris, August 6, 1788

There has been a time when . . . perhaps the esteem of the world was of higher value in my eye than every thing in it. But age, experience, & reflection, preserving to that only its due value, have set a higher on tranquility. The motion of my blood no longer keeps time with the tumult of the world. It leads me to seek for happiness in the lap and love of my family, in the society of my neighbors & my books, in the wholesome occupations of my farm & my affairs, in an interest or affection in every bud that opens, in every breath that blows around me, in an entire freedom of rest or motion, of thought or incogitancy, owing account to myself alone of my hours & actions.

To James Madison, Philadelphia, June 9, 1793

Health

Health must not be sacrificed to learning. A strong body makes the mind strong.

To Peter Carr, Paris, August 19, 1785

Knowledge indeed is desirable, a lovely possession, but I do not scruple to say that health is more so. It is of little consequence to store the mind with science if the body be permitted to become debilitated. If the body be feeble, the mind will not be strong.

To Thomas Mann Randolph, Jr., Paris, August 27, 1786

History

噗 噗

History, by apprizing them of the past, will enable them to judge of the future; it will avail them of the experience of other times and other nations; it will qualify them as judges of the actions and designs of men; it will enable them to know ambition under every disguise it may assume; and knowing it, to defeat its views.

Notes on the State of Virginia, 1782

I learn with great satisfaction that you are about committing to the press the valuable historical and state-papers you have been so long collecting. Time & accident are committing daily havoc on the originals deposited in our public offices. The late war has done the work of centuries in this business. The lost cannot be recovered; but let us save what remains: not by vaults and locks which fence them from the public eye and use, in consigning them to the waste of time, but by such a multiplication of copies, as shall place them beyond the reach of accident.

To Ebenezer Hazard, Philadelphia, February 18, 1791

Wars & contentions indeed fill the pages of history with more matter. But more blest is that nation whose silent course of happiness furnishes nothing for history to say. This is what I ambition for my own country.

To M. Le Comte Diodati, Washington, March 29, 1807

History in general only informs us what bad government is.

To John Norvell, Washington, June 11, 1807

It is truly unfortunate that those engaged in public affairs so rarely make notes of transactions passing within their knowledge. Hence history becomes fable instead of fact. The great outlines may be true, but the incidents and colouring are according to the faith or fancy of the writer.

To William Wirt, Monticello, August 14, 1814

The only exact testimony of a man is his actions, leaving the reader to pronounce on them his own judgment.

To L. H. Girardin, Monticello, March 27, 1815

You say I must go to writing history. While in public life, I had not time: and now that I am retired, I am past the time. To write history requires a whole life of observation, of enquiry, of labor and correction. Its materials are not to be found among the ruins of a decayed memory.

To Josephus B. Stuart, Monticello, May 10, 1817

I feel a much greater interest in knowing what passed two or three thousand years ago, than in what is now passing.

To Nathaniel Macon, Monticello, January 12, 1819

Multiplied testimony, multiplied views will be necessary to give solid establishment to truth. Much is known to one which is not known to another, and no one knows everything. It is the sum of individual knowledge which is to make up the whole truth, and to give its correct current thro' future time.

To William Johnson, Monticello, March 4, 1823

History may distort truth, and will distort it for a time, by the superior efforts at justification of those who are conscious of needing it most. Nor will the opening scenes of our present government be seen in their true aspect until the letters of the day, now held in private hoards, shall be broken up and laid open to public view.

To William Johnson, Monticello, June 12, 1823

It is the duty of every good citizen to use all the opportunities which occur to him, for preserving documents relating to the history of our country.

To Hugh P. Taylor, Monticello, October 4, 1823

Home

🌿 🌿

I had rather be sick in bed there [at home], than in health here.

To Dr. George Gilmer, Philadelphia, May 11, 1792

Honesty

A wise man, if nature has not formed him honest, will yet act as if he were honest: because he will find it the most advantageous & wise part in the long run.

To James Monroe, Paris, March 18, 1785

An honest heart being the first blessing, a knowing head is the second.

To Peter Carr, Paris, August 19, 1785

I cannot act as if all men were unfaithful because some are so; nor believe that all will betray me, because some do. I had rather be the victim of occasional infidelities, than relinquish my general confidence in the honesty of man.

To Thomas Leiper, Monticello, January 1, 1814

Honesty is the 1st chapter in the book of wisdom.

To Nathaniel Macon, Monticello, January 12, 1819

Hope

Hope is sweeter than despair.

To Maria Cosway, Paris, October 12, 1786

I had rather be deceived, than live without hope. It is so sweet! It makes us ride so smoothly over the roughnesses of life. When clambering a mountain, we always hope the hill we are on is the last. But it is the next, and the next, and still the next.

To Maria Cosway, Paris, December 24, 1786

Hospitality

※ ※

You shall find with me a room, bed, & plate with a hearty welcome.

To James Monroe, Paris, December 10, 1784

Call on me in your turn, whenever you come to town: and if it should be about the hour of three, I shall rejoice the more. You will find a bad dinner, a good glass of wine, and a host thankful for your favor, and desirous of encouraging repetitions of it without number, form or ceremony.

To Richard Peters, Philadelphia, June 30, 1791

Human Beings

※ ※

Of all machines ours is the most complicated and inexplicable.

To James Madison, Monticello, August 31, 1783

Human Nature

Mankind soon learn to make interested uses of every right and power which they possess, or may assume.

Notes on the State of Virginia, 1782

Human nature is the same on every side of the Atlantic, and will be alike influenced by the same cause.

Notes on the State of Virginia, 1782

Hunger

Our machine, unsupported by food, is no longer under the control of reason.

To Dr. George Gilmer, Philadelphia, June 28, 1793

Ideas

He who receives an idea from me, receives instruction himself without lessening mine; as he who lights his taper at mine, receives light without darkening me.

To Isaac McPherson, Monticello, August 13, 1813

Idleness

Determine never to be idle. No person will have occasion to complain of the want of time who never loses any. It is wonderful how much may be done if we are always doing.

To Martha Jefferson, Marseilles, May 5, 1787

A mind always employed is always happy. This is the true secret, the grand recipe, for felicity. The idle are the only wretched.

To Martha Jefferson, Toulouse, May 21, 1787

Ignorance

Ignorance is preferable to error; and he is less remote from the truth who believes nothing, than he who believes what is wrong.

Notes on the State of Virginia, 1782

Ignorance & bigotry, like other insanities, are incapable of self-government.

To Marquis de LaFayette, Monticello, May 14, 1817

Indians

The two principles on which our conduct towards the Indians should be founded are justice & fear. After the injuries we have done them, they cannot love us, which leaves us no alternative but that of fear to keep them from attacking us. But justice is what we should never lose sight of, & in time it may recover their esteem.

To Benjamin Hawkins, Paris, August 13, 1786

In truth, the ultimate point of rest & happiness for them is to let our settlements and theirs meet and blend together, to intermix and become one people, incorporating themselves with us as citizens of the U.S. This is what the natural progress of things will of course bring on, and it will be better to promote than to retard it. Surely it will be better for them to be identified with us, and preserved in the occupation of their lands, than be exposed to the many casualties which may endanger them while a separate people.

To Benjamin Hawkins, Washington, February 18, 1803

Indiscretions

It is sometimes difficult to decide whether indiscretions . . . had better be treated with silence, or due notice.

To George Washington, Philadelphia, February 16, 1793

Indolence

Of all the cankers of human happiness none corrodes with so silent, yet so baneful an influence, as indolence.

To Martha Jefferson, Aix en Provence, March 28, 1787

Indulgence

I may have erred at times—no doubt I have errred; this is the law of human nature. For honest errors, however, indulgence may be hoped.

Speech to U.S. Senate, February 28, 1801

Innovation

Great innovations should not be forced on slender majorities.

To Thaddeus Kosciusko, Washington, May 2, 1808

Insult

It should ever be held in mind that insult & war are the consequences of a want of respectability in the national character.

To James Madison, Paris, February 8, 1786

An insult unpunished is the parent of many others.

To Secretary for Foreign Affairs John Jay, Paris, August 23, 1785

One insult pocketed soon produces another.

To President George Washington,
New York, August 28, 1790

Acquiescence under insult is not the way to escape war.

To Henry Tazwell, Monticello, September 13, 1795

Integrity

Rigid integrity is the first and most gainful qualification (in the long run) in every profession.

To John Garland Jefferson, Phialdelphia, February 5, 1791

I am sure that in estimating every man of value either in private or public life, a pure integrity is the quality we take first into calculation, and that learning and talents are only the second. After these come benevolence, good temper &c. But the first is always that sort of integrity which makes a man act in the dark as if it was in the open blaze of day.

To John Garland Jefferson, Philadelphia, June 15, 1792

Intolerance

I never will, by any word or act, bow to the shrine of intolerance.

To Edward Dowse, Washington, April 19, 1803

Intrigue

Nothing is so mistaken as the supposition that a person is to extricate himself from a difficulty, by intrigue, by chicanery, by dissimulation, by trimming, by an untruth, by an injustice. This increases the difficulties tenfold, & those who pursue these methods, get themselves so involved at length that they can turn no way but their infamy becomes more exposed.

To Peter Carr, Paris, August 19, 1785

Jealousy

Doubts or jealousy . . . often beget the facts they fear.

To Albert Gallatin, Washington, October 12, 1806

Jesus

茭 茭

I hold the precepts of Jesus, as delivered by himself, to be the most pure, benevolent, and sublime which have ever been preached to man. I adhere to the principles of the first age; and consider all subsequent innovations as corruptions of his religion, having no foundation in what came from him.

To Jared Sparks, Monticello, November 4, 1820

Judiciary

茭 茭

We find the judiciary on every occasion, still driving us into consolidation. . . . The constitution . . . is a mere thing of wax in the hands of the judiciary, which they may twist and shape into any form they please. It should be remembered as an axiom of eternal truth in politics that whatever power in any government is independent, is absolute.

To Spencer Roane, Poplar Forest, September 6, 1819

The legislative and executive branches may sometimes err, but elections and dependance will bring them to rights. The judiciary branch is the instrument which working, like gravity, without intermission, is to press us at last into one consolidated mass.

To Archibald Thweat, Monticello, January 19, 1821

The great object of my fear is the federal judiciary. That body, like Gravity, ever acting, with noiseless foot, & unalarming advance, gaining ground step by step, and holding what it gains, is ingulphing insidiously the special governments [i.e., the states] into the jaws of that which feeds them.

To Spencer Roane, Monticello, March 9, 1821

It has long however been my opinion, and I have never shrunk from its expression . . . that the germ of dissolution of our federal government is in the constitution of the federal judiciary; an irresponsible body, (for impeachment is scarcely a scare-crow,) working like gravity by night and by day, gaining a little to-day & a little to-morrow, and advancing its noiseless step like a thief, over the field of jurisdiction, until all shall be usurped from the states, & the government of all be consolidated into one.

To C. Hammond, Monticello, August 18, 1821

Justice

All the tranquility, the happiness & security of mankind rest on justice, on the obligation to respect the rights of others.

Opinion on the French Treaties, April 28, 1793

Equal and exact justice to all men, of whatever state or persuasion, religious or political.

First Inaugural Address, March 4, 1801

Justice is the fundamental law of society.

To P. S. DuPont de Nemours, April 24, 1816

Justness

History bears witness to the fact, that a just nation is taken on its word.

Second Inaugural Address, March 4, 1805

Kindness

Above all things lose no occasion of exercising your dispositions to be grateful, to be generous, to be charitable, to be humane, to be true, just, firm, orderly, courageous, &c. Consider every act of this kind as an exercise which will strengthen your moral faculties & increase your worth.

To Peter Carr, Paris, August 10, 1787

Language

⚔ ⚔

Such is become the prostitution of language that sincerity has no longer distinct terms in which to express her own truths.

To George Washington, Philadelphia, January 22, 1783

Style in writing or speaking is formed very early in life while the imagination is warm, & impressions are permanent.

To John Bannister, Jr., Paris, October 15, 1785

Ingenious minds, availing themselves of the imperfection of language, have tortured the expressions out of their plain meaning in order to infer departures from them in practice.

To Isaac Story, Washington, December 5, 1801

Dictionaries are but the depositories of words already legitimated by usage. Society is the work-shop in which new ones are elaborated. When an individual uses a new word, if illformed it is rejected in society, if wellformed, adopted, and, after due time, laid up in the depository of dictionaries.

To John Adams, Monticello, August 15, 1820

Nor am I a friend to a scrupulous purism of style. I readily sacrifice the niceties of syntax to euphony and strength. It is by boldly neglecting the rigorisms of grammar that Tacitus has made himself the strongest writer in the world. The Hypercritics call him barbarous; but I should be sorry to exchange his barbarisms for their wire-drawn purisms.

To Edward Everett, Monticello, February 24, 1823

Laws

We lay it down as a fundamental, that laws, to be just, must give a reciprocation of right; that, without this, they are mere arbitrary rules of conduct, founded in force, and not in conscience.

Notes on the State of Virginia, 1782

The execution of the laws is more important than the making them.

To M. L'Abbe Arnond, Paris, July 19, 1789

Laws are made for men of ordinary understanding, and should therefore be construed by the ordinary rules of common sense. Their meaning is not to be sought for in metaphysical subtleties, which may make any thing mean every thing or nothing, at pleasure.

To William Johnson, Monticello, June 12, 1823

Lawyers

A lawyer without books would be like a workman without tools.

To Thomas Turpin, Shadwell, February 5, 1769

Liberty

The God who gave us life gave us liberty at the same time; the hand of force may destroy, but cannot disjoin them.

A Summary View of the Rights of British America, May 1774

The tree of liberty must be refreshed from time to time with the blood of patriots & tyrants. It is its natural manure.

To William Stephens Smith, Paris, November 13, 1787

The natural progress of things is for liberty to yield, & government to gain ground.

To Edward Carrington, Paris, May 27, 1788

The ground of liberty is to be gained by inches, that we must be contented to secure what we can get from time to time, and eternally press forward for what is yet to get. It takes time to persuade men to do even what is for their own good.

To Charles Clay, Monticello, January 27, 1790

We are not to expect to be translated from despotism to liberty in a feather bed.

To Marquis de LaFayette, New York, April 2, 1790

I would rather be exposed to the inconveniencies attending too much liberty than those attending too small a degree of it.

To Archibald Stuart, Philadelphia, December 23, 1791

This ball of liberty . . . is now so well in motion that it will roll round the globe.

To Tench Coxe, Monticello, June 1, 1795

Timid men . . . prefer the calm of despotism to the boisterous sea of liberty.

To Philip Mazzei, Monticello, April 24, 1796

The last hope of human liberty in this world rests on us. We ought, for so dear a stake, to sacrifice every attachment & every enmity.

To William Duane, Monticello, March 28, 1811

The disease of liberty is catching.

To Marquis de LaFayette, Monticello, December 26, 1820

The boisterous sea of liberty indeed is never without a wave.

To Marquis de Lafayette, Monticello, December 26, 1820

Life

🦋 🦋

The most fortunate of us all in our journey through life frequently meet with calamities and misfortunes which may greatly afflict us; and to fortify our minds against the attacks of these calamities and misfortunes should be one of the principal studies and endeavors of our lives. The only method of doing this is to assure a perfect resignation to the divine will, to consider that whatever does happen, must happen, and that by our uneasiness we cannot prevent the blow before it does fall, but we may add to its force after it has fallen. These considerations and others such as these may enable us in some measure to surmount the difficulties thrown in our way, to bear up with a tolerable degree of patience under this burthen of life, and to proceed with a pious and unshaken resignation till we arrive at our journey's end, where we may deliver up our trust into the hands of him who gave it, and receive such reward as to him shall seem proportioned to our merit.

To John Page, Shadwell, July 15, 1763

Long-Windedness

🦋 🦋

Speeches measured by the hour, die with the hour.

To David Harding, Monticello, April 20, 1824

Love

I wish they had formed us like the birds of the air, able to fly where we please. I would have exchanged for this many of the boasted preeminencies of man. I was so unlucky when very young, as to read the history of Fortunatus. He had a cap of such virtues that when he put it on his head, and wished himself anywhere, he was there. I have been all my life sighing for this cap. Yet if I had it, I question if I should use it but once. I should wish myself with you, and not wish myself away again.

To Maria Cosway, Paris, December 24, 1786

Love is always a consolatory thing.

To Maria Cosway, Paris, May 21, 1789

When wafting on the bosom of the ocean I shall pray it to be as calm and smooth as yours to me.

To Maria Cosway, Paris, May 21, 1789

We think last of those we love most.

To Maria Cosway, Cowes, Isle of Wight, October 14, 1789

The Loyal Minority

A respectable minority is useful as Censors.

To Joel Barlow, Washington, May 3, 1802

Manifest Destiny

Our confederacy must be viewed as the nest from which all America, North & South is to be peopled.

To Archibald Stuart, Paris, January 25, 1786

Marriage

Harmony in the married state is the very first object to be aimed at.

To Mary Jefferson Eppes, Philadelphia, January 7, 1798

Medicine

I acknowledge facts in medicine as far as they go, distrusting only their extension by theory.

To Dr. Benjamin Rush, Poplar Forest, August 17, 1811

Memory

Of all the faculties of the human mind that of Memory is the first which suffers decay from age.

To Benjamin Henry Latrobe, Monticello, July 12, 1812

A life of constant action leaves no time for recording. Always thinking of what is next to be done, what has been done is dismissed and soon obliterated from the memory.

To Horatio Gates Spafford, Monticello, May 11, 1819

Moderation

We never repent of having eaten too little.

To Thomas Jefferson Smith, Monticello, February 21, 1825

Monarchy

I was much an enemy to monarchy before I came to Europe. I am ten thousand times more so since I have seen what they are. There is scarcely an evil known in these countries which may not be traced to their king as its source, nor a good which is not derived from the small fibres of republicanism existing among them.

To George Washington, Paris, May 2, 1788

Money

The want of money cramps every effort.

To George Washington, Richmond, June 11, 1780

Morality

Give up money, give up fame, give up science, give up the earth itself & all it contains rather than do an immoral act. And never suppose that in any possible situation or under any circumstances that it is best for you to do a dishonourable thing however slightly so it may appear to you. Whenever you are to do a thing tho' it can never be known but to yourself, ask yourself how you would act were all the world looking at you, & act accordingly.

To Peter Carr, Paris, August 19, 1785

Morals were too essential to the happiness of man, to be risked on the uncertain combinations of the head. She laid their foundation, therefore, in sentiment, not in science.

To Maria Cosway, Paris, October 12, 1786

We may well admit morality to be the child of the understanding rather than of the senses, when we observe that it becomes dearer to us as the latter weaken, & as the former grows stronger by time & experience till the hour arrives in which all other objects lose all their value.

To Richard Price, Paris, July 11, 1788

I know but one code of morality for man whether acting singly or collectively. He who says I will be a rogue when I act in company with a hundred others but an honest man when I act alone, will be believed in the former assertion, but not in the latter.

To James Madison, Paris, August 28, 1789

We are firmly convinced, and we act on that conviction, that with nations, as with individuals, our interests soundly calculated, will ever be found inseparable from our moral duties.

Second Inaugural Address, March 4, 1805

I sincerely then believe with you in the general existence of a moral instinct. I think it the brightest gem with which the human character is studded; and the want of it as more degrading than the most hideous of the bodily deformities.

To Thomas Law, Poplar Forest, June 13, 1814

He [God] has formed us moral agents. Not that, in the perfection of his state, he can feel pain or pleasure from any thing we may do: he is far above our power; but that we may promote the happiness of those with whom he has placed us in society, by acting honestly towards all, benevolently to those who fall within our way, respecting sacredly their rights, bodily and mental, and cherishing especially their freedom of conscience, as we value our own.

To Miles King, Monticello, September 26, 1814

I fear, from the experience of the last 25 years that morals do not, of necessity, advance hand in hand with the sciences.

To J. Correa de Serra, Monticello, June 28, 1815

Music

If there is a gratification which I envy any people in this world it is to your country its music. This is the favorite passion of my soul, & fortune has cast my lot in a country where it is in a state of deplorable barbarism.

To Giovanni Fabbroni, Williamsburg, June 8, 1778

[Music] will be a companion which will sweeten many hours of life to you.

To Martha Jefferson Randolph, New York, April 4, 1790

Music is invaluable where a person has an ear. Where they have not, it should not be attempted. It furnishes a delightful recreation for the hours of respite from the cares of the day, and lasts us through life.

To Nathaniel Burwell, Monticello, March 14, 1818

Natural Aristocracy

※ ※

I agree with you that there is a natural aristocracy among men. The grounds of this are virtue & talents.

To John Adams, Monticello, October 28, 1813

Neighbors

※ ※

The ill-will of a single neighbor is an immense drawback on the happiness of life, and therefore their good will cannot be bought too dear.

To Martha Jefferson Randolph, Philadelphia, May 8, 1791

Old Age

I find as I grow older, that I love those most whom I loved first.

To Mary Jefferson Bolling, Paris, July 23, 1787

While old men feel sensibly enough their own advance in years, they do not sufficiently recollect it in those whom they have seen young.

To William Short, Philadelphia, January 3, 1793

My health has been always so uniformly firm, that I have for some years dreaded nothing so much as the living too long.

To Benjamin Rush, Washington, December 20, 1801

Being very sensible of bodily decays from advancing years, I ought not to doubt their effect on the mental faculties. To do so would evince either great self-love or little observation of what passes under our eyes: and I shall be fortunate if I am the first to perceive and to obey this admonition of nature.

To Mr. Weaver, Washington, June 7, 1807

A longer period of life was less important, alloyed as the feeble enjoyments of that age are with so much pain.

To Joseph Bringhurst, Washington, February 24, 1808

I find in old age that the impressions of youth are the deepest & most indelible.

To David Campbell, Monticello, January 12, 1810

It is wonderful to me that old men should not be sensible that their minds keep pace with their bodies in the progress of decay. . . . Nothing betrays imbecility so much as the being insensible of it.

To Benjamin Rush, Poplar Forest, August 17, 1811

The hand of age is upon me. The decay of bodily faculties apprises me that those of the mind cannot be unimpaired, had I not still better proofs. Every year counts by increased debility, and departing faculties keep the score. The last year it was the sight, this it is the hearing, the next something else will be going, until all is gone. . . . As a compensation for faculties departed, nature gives me good health, & a perfect resignation to the laws of decay which she has prescribed to all the forms & combinations of matter.

To William Duane, Monticello, October 1, 1812

Our machines have now been running for 70 or 80 years, and we must expect that, worn as they are, here a pivot, there a wheel, now a pinion, next a spring, will be giving way: and however we may tinker them up for awhile, all will at length surcease motion. Our watches, with works of brass and steel, wear out within that period.

To John Adams, Monticello, July 5, 1814

To me every mail, in the departure of some Cotemporary, brings warning to be in readiness myself also, and to cease from new engagements. It is a warning of no alarm. When faculty after faculty is retiring from us, and all the avenues to chearful sensation closing, sight failing now, hearing next, then memory, debility of body, trepitude of mind, nothing remaining but a sickly vegetation, with scarcely the relief of a little loco-motion, the last cannot be but a coup de grace.

To John Melish, Monticello, December 10, 1814

A decline of health, at the age of 76 was naturally to be expected, and is a warning of an event which cannot be distant, and whose approach I contemplate with little concern. For indeed in no circumstance has nature been kinder to us, than in the soft gradations by which she prepares us to part willingly with what we are not destined always to retain. First one faculty is withdrawn and then another, sight, hearing, memory, accuracy, affections, & friends, filched one by one, till we are left among strangers, the mere monuments of times past, and specimens of antiquity for the observation of the curious.

To Horatio Gates Spafford, Monticello, May 11, 1819

Man, like the fruit he eats, has his period of ripeness. Like that too, if he continues longer hanging to the stem, it is but an useless and unsightly appendage.

To Henry Dearborn, Monticello, August 17, 1821

The lapses of memory of an old man, are innocent subjects of compassion, more than of blame.

To John Campbell, Monticello, November 10, 1822

The solitude in which we are left by the death of our friends is one of the great evils of protracted life. When I look back to the days of my youth, it is like looking over a field of battle. All, all dead! and ourselves left alone amidst a new generation whom we know not, and who know not us.

To Francis A. Van Der Kemp, Monticello, January 11, 1825

I know how apt we are to consider those whom we knew long ago, and have not since seen, to be exactly still what they were when we knew them; and to have been stationary in body and mind as they have been in our recollections.

To Edward Livingston, Monticello, March 25, 1825

Opinion

Subject opinion to coercion: whom will you make your inquisitor? Fallible men; men governed by bad passions, by private as well as public reasons. And why subject it to coercion? To produce uniformity. But is uniformity of opinion desirable? No more than of face and stature.

Notes on the State of Virginia, *1782*

When a man whose life has been marked by its candor, has given a latter opinion contrary to a former one, it is probably the result of further inquiry, reflection & conviction.

To Peregrine Fitzhugh, Monticello, April 9, 1797

Even if we differ in principle more than I believe we do, you & I know too well the texture of the human mind, & the slipperiness of human reason, to consider differences of opinion otherwise than differences of form or feature. Integrity of views more than their soundness, is the basis of esteem.

To Elbridge Gerry, Philadelphia, January 26, 1799

Every difference of opinion is not a difference of principle . . . error of opinion may be tolerated where reason is left free to combat it.

First Inaugural Address, March 4, 1801

In every country where man is free to think & to speak, differences of opinion will arise from difference of perception, & the imperfection of reason. But these differences, when permitted, as in this happy country, to purify themselves by free discussion, are but as passing clouds overspreading our land transiently, & leaving our horizon more bright & serene.

To Benjamin Waring, Washington, March 23, 1801

Opinion, & the just maintenance of it, shall never be a crime in my view; nor bring injury on the individual.

To Samuel Adams, Washington, March 29, 1801

I see too many proofs of the imperfection of human reason to entertain wonder or intolerance at any difference of opinion on any subject; and acquiesce in that difference as easily as on a difference of feature or form. Experience having long taught me the reasonableness of mutual sacrifices of opinion among those who are to act together for any common object, and the expediency of doing what good we can; when we cannot do all we would wish.

To John Randolph, Washington, December 1, 1803

I may sometimes differ in opinion from some of my friends, from those whose views are as pure & sound as my own. I censure none, but do homage to every one's right of opinion.

To William Duane, Monticello, March 28, 1811

Difference of opinion leads to inquiry, and inquiry to truth; and that, I am sure, is the ultimate and sincere object of us both. We both value too much the freedom of opinion sanctioned by our constitution, not to cherish its exercise even where in opposition to ourselves.

To P. H. Wendover, Monticello, March 13, 1815

Opinion is power.

To John Adams, Monticello, January 11, 1816

As the Creator has made no two faces alike, so no two minds, and probably no two creeds.

To Timothy Pickering, Monticello, February 27, 1821

These cares however are no longer mine. I resign myself cheerfully to the managers of the ship, and the more contentedly as I am near the end of my voyage. I have learned to be less confident in the conclusions of human reason, and give more credit to the honesty of contrary opinions.

To Edward Livingston, Monticello, April 4, 1824

Opportunity

You live in a country where talents, learning, and honesty are so much called for that every man who possesses these may be what he pleases. Can there be a higher inducement to acquire them at every possible expence of time and labour?

To John Garland Jefferson, Monticello, October 11, 1791

Nature will not give you a second life wherein to atone for the omissions of this.

To Joseph C. Cabell, Monticello, January 31, 1821

Oppression

For what oppression may not a precedent be found in this world.

Notes on the State of Virginia, 1782

Optimism

✹ ✹

I steer my bark with Hope in the head, leaving Fear astern. My hopes indeed sometimes fail; but not oftener than the forebodings of the gloomy.

To John Adams, Monticello, April 8, 1816

Original Intent of the Founders

✹ ✹

The constitution on which our Union rests, shall be administered by me according to the safe and honest meaning contemplated by the plain understanding of the people of the United States, at the time of its adoption: a meaning to be found in the explanations of those who advocated, not of those who opposed it, and who opposed it merely lest the constructions should be applied which they denounced as possible. These explanations are preserved in the publications of the time, and are too recent in the memories of most men to admit of question.

To Messrs. Eddy, Russel, Thurber, Wheaton, and Smyth,
Washington, March 27, 1801

Some men look at Constitutions with sanctimonious reverence; & deem them, like the ark of the covenant, too sacred to be touched. They ascribe to the men of the preceding age a wisdom more than human, and suppose what they did to be beyond amendment. I knew that age well: I belonged to it, and labored with it. It deserved well of its country. It was very like the present, but without the experience of the present: and 40 years of experience in government is worth a century of book-reading: and this they would say themselves, were they to rise from the dead. I am certainly not an advocate for frequent & untried changes in laws and constitutions. I think moderate imperfections had better be borne with; because when once known, we accomodate ourselves to them, and find practical means of correcting their ill effects. But I know also that laws and institutions must go hand in hand with the progress of the human mind. As that becomes more developed, more enlightened, as new discoveries are made, new truths disclosed, and manners and opinions change with the change of circumstances, institutions must advance also, and keep pace with the times. We might as well require a man to wear still the coat which fitted him when a boy, as civilized society to remain ever under the regimen of their barbarous ancestors.

To Samuel Kercheval, Monticello, July 12, 1816

Pain

THE HEAD SPEAKING

The art of life is the art of avoiding pain; and he is the best pilot who steers clearest of the rocks and shoals with which it is beset. Pleasure is always before us, but misfortune is at our side; while running after that, this arrests us.

We have no rose without its thorn; no pleasure without alloy. It is the law of our existence, and we must acquiesce. It is the condition annexed to all our pleasures, not by us who receive, but by him who gives them.

To Maria Cosway, Paris, October 12, 1786

Parenting

🦗 🦗

Is it [parental love] not the strongest affection known? Is it not greater than even that of self-preservation?

A Bill for Proportioning Crime and Punishment, November 1778

The post which a parent may take most advantageous for his child is that of his bosom friend.

To John Banister, Sr., Paris, February 7, 1787

Nature knows no laws between parent and child, but the will of the parent.

To Thomas Mann Randolph, Monticello, October 22, 1790

The article of discipline is the most difficult in American education. Premature ideas of independence, too little repressed by parents, beget a spirit of insubordination, which is the great obstacle.

To Dr. Thomas Cooper, Monticello, November 2, 1822

Passion

All men who have attended to the workings of the human mind, who have seen the false colours under which passion sometimes dresses the actions and motives of others, have seen also these passions subsiding with time and reflection, dissipating, like mists before the rising sun, and restoring to us the sight of all things in their true shape and colours.

To John Adams, Monticello, October 12, 1823

Patriotism

That my country should be served is the first wish of my heart.

To the Mayor, Recorder & Aldermen of Norfolk, November 25, 1789

The man who loves his country on its own account, and not merely for its trappings of interest or power, can never be divorced from it; can never refuse to come forward when he finds that she is engaged in dangers which he has the means of warding off.

To Elbridge Gerry, Philadelphia, June 21, 1797

The first object of my heart is my own country. In that is embarked my family, my fortune, & my own existence. I have not one farthing of interest, nor one fibre of attachment out of it, nor a single motive of preference of any one nation to another, but in proportion as they are more or less friendly to us.

To Elbridge Gerry, Philadelphia, January 26, 1799

My affections were first for my own country, and then generally for all mankind.

To Thomas Law, Monticello, January 15, 1811

Peace

✣ ✣

Peace and friendship with all mankind is our wisest policy: and I wish we may be permitted to pursue them. But the temper and the folly of our enemies may not leave this in our choice.

To C.W.F. Dumas, Paris, May 6, 1786

We love & we value peace: we know its blessings from experience. We abhor the follies of war, & are not untried in its distresses & calamities.

*To William Carmichael and William Short,
Philadelphia, June 30, 1793*

As to myself, I love peace, and I am anxious that we should give the world still another useful lesson, by showing to them other modes of punishing injuries than by war, which is as much a punishment to the punisher as to the sufferer.

To Tench Coxe, Monticello, May 1, 1794

Peace & justice shall be the polar stars of the American societies.

To J. Correa de Serra, Monticello, October 24, 1820

Perseverance

An indifferent measure carried through with perseverance is better than a good one taken up only at intervals.

To Timothy Pickering, Richmond, September 6, 1780

Persuasiveness

Persuasion, perseverance, and patience are the best advocates on questions depending on the will of others.

To James Heaton, Monticello, May 20, 1826

Pessimism

There are indeed (who might say Nay) gloomy & hypocondriac minds, inhabitants of diseased bodies, disgusted with the present, & despairing of the future; always counting that the worst will happen, because it may happen. To these I say How much pain have cost us the evils which have never happened?

To John Adams, Monticello, April 8, 1816

Petitions

🐝 🐝

The right of our fellow citizens to represent to the public functionaries their opinion on proceedings interesting to them, is unquestionably a constitutional right, often useful, sometimes necessary, and will always be respectfully acknowledged by me.

To New Haven Merchants, Washington, July 12, 1801

Pleasure

🐝 🐝

I do not agree that an age of pleasure is no compensation for a moment of pain.

To John Adams, Monticello, August 1, 1816

Poetry

Misery is often the parent of the most affecting touches in poetry. . . . Love is the peculiar œstrum of the poet.

Notes on the State of Virginia, 1782

Politeness

With respect to what are termed political manners, without sacrificing too much the sincerity of language, I would wish my countrymen to adopt just so much of European politeness as to be ready to make all those little sacrifices of self which really render European manners amiable, and relieve society from the disagreeable scenes to which rudeness often exposes it.

To Charles Bellini, Paris, September 30, 1785

In truth, politeness is artificial good humor, it covers the natural want of it, & ends by rendering habitual a substitute nearly equivalent to the real virtue. It is the practice of sacrificing to those whom we meet in society all the little conveniences & preferences which will gratify them, & deprive us of nothing worth a moment's consideration; it is the giving a pleasing & flattering turn to our expressions which will conciliate others, and make them pleased with us as well as themselves. How cheap a price for the good will of another!

To Thomas Jefferson Randolph, Washington, November 24, 1808

Political Dissension

Political dissension is doubtless a less evil than the lethargy of despotism, but still it is a great evil, and it would be as worthy the efforts of the patriot as of the philosopher, to exclude its influence, if possible, from social life.

To Thomas Pinckney, Philadelphia, May 29, 1797

Political Enemies

Let them have justice, and protection against personal violence, but no favor. Powers & preeminences conferred on them are daggers put into the hands of assassins, to be plunged into our own bosoms in the moment the thrust can go home to the heart. Moderation can never reclaim them. They deem it timidity, & despise without fearing the tameness from which it flows.

To Henry Dearborne, Poplar Forest, August 14, 1811

I never suffered a political to become a personal difference.

To Timothy Pickering, Monticello, February 27, 1821

Political Parties

🌿 🌿

I am not a Federalist, because I never submitted the whole system of my opinions to the creed of any party of men whatever in religion, in philosophy, in politics, or in any thing else where I was capable of thinking for myself. Such an addiction is the last degradation of a free and moral agent. If I could not go to heaven but with a party, I would not go there at all.

To Francis Hopkinson, Paris, March 13, 1789

Men by their constitutions are naturally divided into two parties: 1. Those who fear and distrust the people, and wish to draw all powers from them into the hands of the higher classes. 2nly. Those who identify themselves with the people, have confidence in them, cherish and consider them as the most honest & safe, altho' not the most wise depository of the public interests. In every country these two parties exist, and in every one where they are free to think, speak, and write, they will declare themselves. Call them therefore liberals and serviles, Jacobins and Ultras, whigs and tories, republicans and federalists, aristocrats & democrats, or by whatever name you please, they are the same parties still, and pursue the same object.

The last appellation of aristocrats and democrats is the true one expressing the essence of all.

To Henry Lee, Monticello, August 10, 1824

Pragmatism

♜ ♜

I have ever thought that forms should yield to whatever should facilitate business.

To James Monroe, Washington, July 11, 1801

Praise

♜ ♜

Go on deserving applause, and you will be sure to meet with it: and the way to deserve it is, to be good, & to be industrious.

To John W. Eppes, Paris, July 28, 1787

Approbation of my fellow citizens is the richest reward I can receive.

To Richard M. Johnson, Washington, March 10, 1808

Precedents

✣ ✣

A departure from principle in one instance becomes a precedent for a 2d., that 2d. for a 3d. and so on, till the bulk of the society is reduced to be mere automatons of misery, to have no sensibilities left but for sinning and suffering.

To Samuel Kercheval, Monticello, July 12, 1816

The Presidency

✣ ✣

The second office of this government is honorable & easy, the first is but a splendid misery.

To Elbridge Gerry, Philadelphia, May 13, 1797

The Press

✣ ✣

I am persuaded myself that the good sense of the people will always be found to be the best army. . . . The basis of our governments being the opinion of the people, the very first object should be to keep that right; and were it left to me to decide whether we should have a government without newspapers, or

newspapers without a government, I should not hesi-
tate a moment to prefer the latter.

To Edward Carrington, Paris, January 16, 1787

Newspapers . . . serve as chimnies to carry off noxious
vapors and smoke.

To Thaddeus Kosciusko, Washington, April 2, 1802

I deplore with you the putrid state into which our
newspapers have passed, and the malignity, the vul-
garity, & mendacious spirit of those who write for
them.

To Walter Jones, Monticello, January 2, 1814

A truth now and then projecting into the ocean of
newspaper lies, serves like headlands to correct our
course. Indeed my scepticism as to every thing I see
in a newspaper makes me indifferent whether I ever
see one.

To James Monroe, Monticello, January 1, 1815

If a nation expects to be ignorant & free, in a state of
civilization, it expects what never was & never will be.
The functionaries of every government have propen-
sities to command at will the liberty & property of
their constituents. There is no safe deposit for these
but with the people themselves; nor can they be safe
with them without information. Where the press is
free and every man able to read, all is safe.

To Charles Yancey, Monticello, January 6, 1816

This formidable censor of the public functionaries, by arraigning them at the tribunal of public opinion, produces reform peaceably, which must otherwise be done by revolution.

To M. Coray, Monticello, October 31, 1823

The only security of all is in a free press. The force of public opinion cannot be resisted, when permitted freely to be expressed. The agitation it produces must be submitted to. It is necessary to keep the waters pure.

To Marquis de LaFayette, Monticello, November 4, 1823

Pride

Pride costs us more than hunger, thirst and cold.

To Thomas Jefferson Smith, Monticello, February 21, 1825

Principles

Ꮬ Ꮬ

When principles are well understood their application is less embarrassing.

To Gouverneur Morris, Philadelphia, December 30, 1792

An unprincipled man, let his other fitnesses be what they will, ought never to be employed.

To Dr. George Gilmer, Philadelphia, June 28, 1793

True wisdom does not lie in mere practice without principle.

To John Adams, Monticello, October 14, 1816

Privacy

A room to myself, if it be but a barrack, is indispensable.

To James Madison, Monticello, August 31, 1783

Progress

Truth advances, & error recedes step by step only; and to do to our fellow-men the most good in our power, we must lead where we can, follow where we cannot, and still go with them, watching always the favorable moment for helping them to another step.

To Thomas Cooper, Monticello, October 7, 1814

Public Censure

My great wish is to go on in a strict but silent performance of my duty: to avoid attracting notice & to keep my name out of newspapers, because I find the pain of a little censure, even when it is unfounded, is more acute than the pleasure of much praise.

To Francis Hopkinson, Paris, March 13, 1789

Public Confidence

It would be a dangerous delusion were a confidence in the man of our choice to silence our fears for the safety of our rights: that confidence is everywhere the parent of despotism—free government is founded in jealousy, and not in confidence; it is jealousy and not confidence which prescribes limited constitutions, to bind down those whom we are obliged to trust with power. . . . In questions of power, then, let no more be heard of confidence in man, but bind him down from mischief by the chains of the Constitution.

Kentucky Resolutions, October 1798

It is not wisdom alone, but public confidence in that wisdom, which can support an administration.

To President James Monroe, Monticello, July 18, 1824

Public Credit

The existence of a nation, having no credit, is always precarious.

To James Madison, Paris, May 3, 1788

Public Debt

I, however, place economy among the first and most important of republican virtues, and public debt as the greatest of the dangers to be feared.

To William Plumer, Monticello, July 21, 1816

I am for a government rigorously frugal & simple, applying all the possible savings of the public revenue to the discharge of the national debt.

To Elbridge Gerry, Philadelphia, January 26, 1799

Public Opinion

The advantage of public opinion; is like that of the weathergauge in a naval action.

To James Monroe, Monticello, January 1, 1815

When public opinion changes, it is with the rapidity of thought.

To Charles Yancey, Monticello, January 6, 1816

Public Service

I may think public service & private misery inseparably linked together.

To James Monroe, Monticello, May 20, 1782

Honesty, knowledge & industry are the qualities which will lead you to the highest employments of your country, & to its highest esteem, and with these to that satisfaction which renders life pleasant, & death secure.

To Thomas Mann Randolph, Jr., Paris, November 25, 1785

Racism

Deep-rooted prejudices entertained by the whites; ten thousand recollections, by the blacks, of the injuries they have sustained; new provocations; the real distinctions which nature has made; and many other circumstances, will divide us into parties, and produce convulsions, which will probably never end but in the extermination of the one or the other race.

Notes on the State of Virginia, *1782*

Reason

Reason and persuasion are the only practicable instruments. To make way for these, free inquiry must be indulged; and how can we wish others to indulge it while we refuse it ourselves.

Notes on the State of Virginia, 1782

Your own reason is the only oracle given you by heaven, and you are answerable not for the rightness but uprightness of the decision.

To Peter Carr, Paris, August 10, 1787

Reason, not rashness, is the only means of bringing our fellow citizens to their true minds.

To Nicholas Lewis, Philadelphia, January 30, 1799

Truth & reason are eternal. They have prevailed. And they will eternally prevail, however, in times & places, they may be overborne for a while by violence military, civil, or ecclesiastical.

To Samuel Knox, Monticello, February 12, 1810

Every man's own reason must be his oracle.

To Benjamin Rush, Monticello, March 6, 1813

Man, once surrendering his reason, has no remaining guard against absurdities the most monstrous, and like a ship without rudder, is the sport of every wind. With such persons, gullability, which they call faith, takes the helm from the hand of reason and the mind becomes a wreck.

To James Smith, Monticello, December 8, 1822

Rebellion

I hold it that a little rebellion now and then is a good thing, & as necessary in the political world as storms in the physical. Unsuccessful rebellions indeed generally establish the incroachments on the rights of the people which have produced them. An observation of this truth should render honest republican governors so mild in their punishment of rebellions, as not to discourage them too much. It is a medicine necessary for the sound health of government.

To James Madison, Paris, January 30, 1787

The spirit of resistance to government is so valuable on certain occasions, that I wish it to be always kept alive. It will often be exercised when wrong, but better so than not to be exercised at all. I like a little rebellion now & then. It is like a storm in the Atmosphere.

To Abigail Adams, Paris, February 22, 1787

God forbid we should ever be 20 years without such a rebellion. The people can not be all, & always, well informed. The part which is wrong will be discontented in proportion to the importance of the facts they misconceive. If they remain quiet under such misconceptions, it is lethargy, the forerunner of death to the public liberty. We have had 13 states independent for 11 years. There has been one rebellion [Shays's Rebellion]. That comes to one rebellion in a century and a half for each state. What country before ever existed a century & a half without a rebellion? & what country can preserve its liberties, if their rulers are not warned from time to time that their people preserve the spirit of resistance? Let them take arms. The remedy is to set them right as to facts, pardon & pacify them. What signify a few lives lost in a century or two? The tree of liberty must be refreshed from time to time with the blood of patriots & tyrants. It is its natural manure.

To William Stephens Smith, Paris, November 13, 1787

Reclusiveness

Nobody will care for him who cares for nobody.

To Maria Cosway, Paris, October 12, 1786

Reform

The hole & the patch should be commensurate.

To James Madison, Paris, June 20, 1787

Religion

Believing with you that religion is a matter which lies solely between Man & his God, that he owes account to none other for his faith or his worship, that the legitimate powers of government reach actions only, & not opinions, I contemplate with sovereign reverence that act of the whole American people which declared that their legislature should "make no law respecting an establishment of religion, or prohibiting the free exercise thereof," thus building a wall of separation between Church & State. Adhering to this expression of the supreme will of the nation in behalf of the rights of conscience, I shall see with sincere satisfaction the progress of those sentiments which tend to restore to man all his natural rights, convinced he has no natural right in opposition to his social duties.

To the Baptist Association of Danbury, Conn., January 1, 1802

Religion is not the subject for you & me; neither of us knows the religious opinions of the other: that is a matter between our maker & ourselves.

To Thomas Leiper, Washington, January 21, 1809

The subject of religion, a subject on which I have ever been most scrupulously reserved, I have considered it as a matter between every man and his maker, in which no other, & far less the public had a right to intermeddle.

To Richard Rush, Monticello, May, 31, 1813

Nay, we have heard it said that there is not a quaker or a baptist, a presbyterian or an episcopalian, a catholic or a protestant in heaven: that, on entering that gate, we leave those badges of schism behind, and find ourselves united in those principles only in which god has united us all.

To Miles King, Monticello, September 26, 1814

I have ever thought religion a concern purely between our god and our consciences, for which we were accountable to him, and not to the priests. I never told my own religion, nor scrutinised that of another. I never attempted to make a convert, nor wished to change another's creed . . . it is in our lives, and not from our words, that our religion must be read.

To Mrs. M. Harrison Smith, Monticello, August 6, 1816

In that branch of religion which regards the moralities of life, and the duties of a social being, which teaches us to love our neighbors as ourselves, and to do good to all men, I am sure that you & I do not differ. We probably differ on that which relates to the dogmas of theology, the foundation of all sectarianism, and on which no two sects dream alike; for if they did they would then be of the same. You say you are a Calvinist. I am not. I am of a sect by myself, as far as I know.

To Ezra Stiles, Monticello, June 25, 1819

Republican Government

The true foundation of republican government is the equal right of every citizen in his person & property, & in their management.

To Samuel Kercheval, Monticello, July 12, 1816

Reputation

A determination never to do what is wrong, prudence, and good humor, will go far towards securing to you the estimation of the world.

To Thomas Jefferson Randolph, Washington, November 24, 1808

Resistance

When patience has begotten false estimates of its motives, when wrongs are pressed because it is believed they will be borne, resistance becomes morality.

To Madame de Stael de Holstein, Washington, July 16, 1807

Responsibility

Responsibility weighs with its heaviest force on a single head.

To Samuel Kerchival, Monticello, July 12, 1816

Retirement

I look to that period with the longing of a wave-worn mariner, who has at length the land in view, & shall count the days & hours which still lie between me & it.

To George Washington, Monticello, September 9, 1792

I now contemplate the approach of that moment with the fondness of a sailor who has land in view.

To Thomas Pinckney, Philadelphia, November 8, 1792

My books, my family, my friends, & my farm, furnish more than enough to occupy me the remainder of my life, & of that tranquil occupation most analogous to my physical & moral constitution.

To Monsieur Odit, Monticello, October 14, 1795

Never did a prisoner, released from his chains, feel such relief as I shall on shaking off the shackles of power. Nature intended me for the tranquill pursuits of science, by rendering them my supreme delight. But the enormities of the times in which I have lived, have forced me to take a part in resisting them, and to commit myself on the boisterous ocean of political passions. I thank god for the opportunity of retiring from them.

To P. S. Dupont de Nemours, Washington, March 2, 1809

Rights

We hold these truths to be self-evident, that all men are created equal; that they are endowed by their Creator with certain unalienable Rights, that among these are Life, Liberty and the pursuit of Happiness.—That to secure these rights, Governments are instituted among Men, deriving their just powers from the consent of the governed,—that whenever any Form of Government becomes destructive of these ends, it is the Right of the People to alter or to abolish it; and to institute new government, laying its foundation on such principles and organizing its powers in such form, as to them shall seem most likely to effect their Safety and Happiness.

Declaration of Independence, July 1776

Nothing then is unchangeable but the inherent and unalienable rights of man.

To John Cartwright, Monticello, June 5, 1824

Rules

The forming a general rule requires great caution.

To George Washington, 1793

There is no rule without exceptions: but it is false reasoning which converts exceptions into the general rule.

To Thomas Law, Poplar Forest, June 13, 1814

Sacrifice

To save permanent rights, temporary sacrifices were necessary.

To William Eustis, Washington, January 14, 1809

Silence

Remember that we often repent of what we have said, but never of that which we have not.

To Gideon Granger, Monticello, March 9, 1814

Sincerity

It is a proof of sincerity, which I value above all things; as, between those who practise it, falsehood & malice work their efforts in vain.

To William Duane, Washington, March 22, 1806

Slander

There is not a truth on earth which I fear or would disguise. But secret slanders cannot be disarmed because they are secret.

To William Duane, Washington, March 22, 1806

Slavery

Can the liberties of a nation be thought secure when we have removed their only firm basis, a conviction in the minds of the people that these liberties are of the gift of god? That they are not to be violated but with his wrath? Indeed I tremble for my country when I reflect that god is just; that his justice cannot sleep forever.

Notes on the States of Virginia, 1782

There must doubtless be an unhappy influence on the manners of our people produced by the existence of slavery among us. The whole commerce between master and slave is a perpetual exercise of the most boisterous passions, the most unremitting despotism on the one part, and degrading submissions on the other.

Notes on the State of Virginia, 1782

Virginia. This is the next state to which we may turn our eyes for the interesting spectacle of justice in conflict with avarice & oppression: a conflict wherein the sacred side is gaining daily recruits from the influx into office of young men grown & growing up. These have sucked in the principles of liberty as it were with their mother's milk, and it is to them I look with anxiety to turn the fate of this question.

To Richard Price, Paris, August 7, 1785

What a stupendous, what an incomprehensible machine is man! Who can endure toil, famine, stripes, imprisonment or death itself in vindication of his own liberty, and the next moment be deaf to all those motives whose power supported him thro' his trial, and inflict on his fellow men a bondage, one hour of which is fraught with more misery than ages of that which he rose in rebellion to oppose. But we must await with patience the workings of an overruling providence, and hope that that is preparing the deliverance of these our suffering brethren. When the measure of their tears shall be full, when their groans shall have involved heaven itself in darkness, doubtless a god of justice will awaken to their distress, and by diffusing light and liberality among their oppressors, or at length by his exterminating thunder, manifest his attention to the things of this world, and that they are not left to the guidance of a blind fatality.

To Jean Nicolas Demeunier, Paris, June 26 1786

Whatever may have been the circumstances which influenced our forefathers to permit the introduction of personal bondage into any part of these states, & to participate in the wrongs committed on an unoffending quarter of the globe, we may rejoice that such circumstances, & such a sense of them, exist no longer. It is honorable to the nation at large that their legislature availed themselves of the first practicable moment for arresting the progress of this great moral & political error: and I sincerely pray with you, my friends, that all the members of the human family may, in the time prescribed by the Father of us all, find themselves securely established in the enjoyments of life, liberty, & happiness.

To Messrs. Thomas, Ellicot, and Others, November 13, 1807

The love of justice & the love of country plead equally the cause of these people [black slaves], and it is a mortal reproach to us that they should have pleaded it so long in vain, and should have produced not a single effort, nay I fear not much serious willingness to relieve them & ourselves from our present condition of moral and political reprobation.

To Edward Coles, Monticello, Monticello, August 25, 1814

There is nothing I would not sacrifice to a practicable plan of abolishing every vestige of this moral and political depravity.

To Thomas Cooper, Monticello, September 10, 1814

But this momentous question [the Missouri Compromise], like a fire bell in the night, awakened and filled me with terror. I considered it at once as the knell of the Union. It is hushed indeed for the moment. But this is a reprieve only, not a final sentence. A geographical line, coinciding with a marked principle, moral and political, once conceived and held up to the angry passions of men, will never be obliterated; and every new irritation will mark it deeper and deeper. I can say with conscious truth that there is not a man on earth who would sacrifice more than I would to relieve us from this heavy reproach, in any *practicable* way. The cession of that kind of property, for so it is misnamed, is a bagatelle which would not cost me a second thought, if, in that way, a general emancipation and *expatriation* could be effected: and, gradually, and with due sacrifices, I think it might be. But as it is, we have the wolf by the ear, and we can neither hold him, nor safely let him go. Justice is in one scale, and self-preservation in the other.

To John Holmes, Monticello, April 22, 1820

Statesmanship

The man who is dishonest as a statesman would be a dishonest man in any station.

To George Logan, Monticello, November 12, 1816

Steadfastness

Our part then is to pursue with steadiness what is right, turning neither to right nor left for the intrigues or popular delusions of the day, assured that the public approbation will in the end be with us.

To John Breckinridge, Monticello, April 9, 1822

Sympathy

When languishing then under disease, how grateful is the solace of our friends! How are we penetrated with their assiduities & attentions! How much are we supported by their encouragements & kind offices! When Heaven has taken from us some object of our love, how sweet is it to have a bosom whereon to recline our heads, & into which we may pour the torrents of our tears! Grief, with such a comfort, is almost a luxury!

To Maria Cosway, Paris, October 12, 1786

Taxation

No experience has shewn that a gift of perpetual revenue secures a perpetual return of duty or of kind disposition.

Resolutions in the Continental Congress, February 1775

If we can prevent the government from wasting the labors of the people, under the pretense of taking care of them, they must become happy.

To Thomas Cooper, January 29, 1802

The frequent recurrence of this chastening operation can alone restrain the propensity of governments to enlarge expence beyond income.

To Albert Gallatin, Monticello, December 26, 1820

Thrift

We must make our election between *economy & liberty*, or *profusion and servitude*.

To Samuel Kerchival, Monticello, July 12, 1816

Never spend your money before you have it.

To Thomas Jefferson Smith, Monticello, February 21, 1825

Time

Consider how little time is left you, and how much you have to attain in it, and that every moment you lose of it is lost for ever.

To Francis Eppes, Monticello, October 6, 1820

Time is now the most pressing and precious thing in the world to you, and the greatest injury which can possibly be done you is to waste what remains.

To Francis Eppes, Poplar Forest, December 13, 1820

Tobacco

It is a culture productive of infinite wretchedness.

Notes on the State of Virginia, 1782

Tranquility

Tranquility is the old man's milk.

To Edward Rutledge, Philadelphia, June 24, 1797

Tranquility, at my age, is the balm of life.

To P. H. Wendover, Monticello, March 13, 1815

To procure tranquility of mind we must avoid desire & fear, the two principal diseases of the mind.

To William Short, Monticello, October 31, 1819

Travel

Travelling . . . makes men wiser, but less happy.

To Peter Carr, Paris, August 10, 1787

Time, absence, & comparison render my own country much dearer, and give a lustre to all it contains which I did not before know that it merited.

To Wilson Miles Cary, Paris, August 12, 1787

When you are doubting whether a thing is worth the trouble of going to see, recollect that you will never again be so near it, that you may repent the not having seen it, but can never repent having seen it.

Hints on European Travel, Paris, June 1788

Trees

⚘ ⚘

I never before knew the full value of trees. My house is entirely embosomed in high plane trees, with good grass below, & under them I breakfast, dine, write, read, & receive my company. What would I not give that the trees planted nearest round the house at Monticello were full grown.

To Martha Jefferson Randolph, Philadelphia, July 7, 1793

Truth

⚘ ⚘

It is error alone which needs the support of government. Truth can stand by itself.

Notes on the State of Virginia, 1782

It is of great importance to set a resolution, not to be shaken, never to tell an untruth. There is no vice so mean, so pitiful, so contemptible: & he who permits himself to tell a lie once, finds it much easier to do it a second & third time, till at length it becomes habitual, he tells lies without attending to it, & truths without the world's believing him. This falsehood of the tongue leads to that of the heart, & in time depraves all its good dispositions.

To Peter Carr, Paris, August 19, 1785

Truth, between candid minds, can never do harm.

To John Adams, Philadelphia, July 17, 1791

The man who fears no truths has nothing to fear from lies.

To George Logan, 1816

We are not afraid to follow truth wherever it may lead, nor to tolerate any error so long as reason is left free to combat it.

To William Roscoe, Monticello, December 27, 1820

All should be laid open to you without reserve, for there is not a truth existing which I fear, or would wish unknown to the whole world.

To Henry Lee, Monticello, May 15, 1826

Tyranny

The time to guard against corruption and tyranny, is before they shall have gotten hold of us. It is better to keep the wolf out of the fold, than to trust to drawing his teeth and talons after he shall have entered.

Notes on the State of Virginia, *1782*

I have sworn upon the altar of god eternal hostility against every form of tyranny over the mind of man.

To Benjamin Rush, Monticello, September 23, 1800

Unity

A nation united can never be conquered.

To John Adams, Monticello, January 11, 1816

Vigilance

Let the eye of vigilance never be closed.

To Spencer Roane, Monticello, March 9, 1821

Virtue

Encourage all your virtuous dispositions, & exercise them whenever an opportunity arises, being assured that they will gain strength by exercise as a limb of the body does, & that exercise will make them habitual. From the practice of the purest virtue you may be assured you will derive the most sublime comforts in every moment of life, & in the moment of death.

To Peter Carr, Paris, August 19, 1785

Walking

The object of walking is to relax the mind. You should therefore not permit yourself even to think while you walk. But direct your attention by the objects surrounding you. Walking is the best possible exercise. Habituate yourself to walk very far.

To Peter Carr, Paris, August 19, 1785

Of all exercises walking is best. . . . No one knows, till he tries, how easily a habit of walking is acquired. A person who never walked three miles will in the course of a month become able to walk 15 or 20 without fatigue. I have known some great walkers & had particular accounts of many more; and I never knew or heard of one who was not healthy & long lived. This species of exercise therefore is much to be advised.

To Thomas Mann Randolph, Jr., Paris, August 27, 1786

War

I abhor war, and view it as the greatest scourge of mankind.

To Elbridge Gerry, Philadelphia, May 13, 1797

Whensoever hostile agressions . . . require resort to war, we must meet our duty and convince the world that we are just friends and brave enemies.

To Andrew Jackson, December 3, 1806

Trophies obtained by the blood-stained steel, or the tattered flags of the tented field, will never be envied.

To the Republican Citizens of Washington County, Maryland,
Monticello, March 31, 1809

Wine

I rejoice, as a Moralist, at the prospect of a reduction of the duties on wine, by our national legislature. It is an error to view a tax on that liquor as merely a tax on the rich. It is a prohibition of its use to the middling class of our citizens, and a condemnation of them to the poison of whiskey, which is desolating their houses. No nation is drunken where wine is cheap; and none sober, where the dearness of wine substitutes ardent spirits as the common beverage. It is in truth the only antidote to the bane of whiskey. Fix but the duty at the rate of other merchandise, and we can drink wine here as cheaply as we do grog; and who will not prefer it? Its extended use will carry health and comfort to a much enlarged circle. Every one in easy circumstances (as the bulk of our citizens are) will prefer it to the poison to which they are now driven by their government.

To M. De Neuville, Monticello, December 13, 1818

Wisdom

❦ ❦

Wisdom, I know, is social. She seeks her fellows. But Beauty is jealous, and illy bears the presence of a rival.

To Abigail Adams, Paris, September 25, 1785

Women

❦ ❦

Nothing can be more unmanly than to treat a lady superciliously.

To Peter Carr, Annapolis, December 11, 1783

Youth

❦ ❦

It is while we are young that the habit of industry is formed. If not then, it never is afterwards. The fortune of our lives therefore depends on employing well the short period of youth.

To Martha Jefferson, Aix en Provence, March 28, 1787

INDEX